THANKS LIVING

THANKS LIVING

*How to Overcome Life's Trials through
the Power of Gratitude*

JEFF DAWS
& CHESNEE DORSEY

EDITED BY JOE OLIVER

XULON PRESS

Xulon Press
2301 Lucien Way #415
Maitland, FL 32751
407.339.4217
www.xulonpress.com

Edited by Joe Oliver.

Paperback ISBN-13: 978-1-6628-5461-3
Ebook ISBN-13: 978-1-6628-5462-0

CONTENTS

Dedication. ix

1. Gratitude 1

2. Grateful That God Is for Me 11

3. Gratitude: The Stress Reliever. 21

4. Grateful That God Is with Me. 33

5. Love Completely through Gratitude .43

6. We Can Be Grateful Because God Loves Us. 55

7. Expressing Gratitude 63

Dedication

We dedicate this book to Dr. John C. Maxwell.

John, through your teachings on leadership, you have enabled people like us to go far beyond what we dreamed was possible. We titled this book *Thanks Living* because of your influence in our lives. Through your books and videos, you have taught us that our attitude will determine our altitude, that leadership begins by leading ourselves first, and that when leaders get better, everything gets better around them. You have shown us how to escape the traps of small and negative thinking. In truth, we never would have attempted to write this book had it not been for your challenge to all leaders to bet on themselves and to put their trust in God.

John, we are better people, parents, and pastors because of your investment in our lives. And from the depths of our hearts, we say "Thank you" for challenging us to dream bigger, think smarter, and pray harder to rise above our doubts and fears to achieve what is seemingly impossible. We represent the countless people who you have taught from a distance. You may not know us by name, but you have changed our lives.

Chapter 1

Gratitude

from Jeff

I t was like a scene from an apocalyptic movie. From the largest cities to the smallest towns, normally crowded streets all across the world were deserted. Gated and locked up storefronts looked out at empty sidewalks. Subway trains and buses sat eerily still and unused. Even Time Square, one of the most visited destinations in the world, looked like a ghost town, with only a few random pieces of paper blowing around the solitary scene. A cardboard sign, hastily written in marker and taped to a store window, told the story: "Closed due to Covid."

As I sat at home, like billions of everyday people all over the world, watching the infection numbers and death toll continuously rise to scary new heights, I felt tense and uncertain about the future–the future of our country, the future of our economy, the future of our government, the future of my friends and family, the future of their jobs and businesses, and the future of my church.

In the short span of weeks, it was like the whole world had been turned upside down and that we were now all living in a strange, unfamiliar world. We were now separated from one another by lockdowns and a "social" distance of six feet. We became anxious, nervous, and angry as we waited long hours in lines, hoping that the store hadn't run out of what we needed to buy, just to find out that the store *had* run out of what we needed to buy.

And the longer the virus lingered the worse we as a community became divided. It seemed like every day, a new controversy rose up, and people who had been friendly toward one another prior to the pandemic, erupted in fury at each other over any number of topics and battled it out on social media.

I felt shaken and deeply sad. It felt like the world had been forever turned inside out and that nothing would ever be the same again.

How Do We Go On?

When your life is in turmoil and it seems like there is no way to continue forward, what can get you through?

Well, my friend, my answer to that question is *gratitude*.

This answer may seem confusing at first. After all, how can someone be *grateful* for something that has been hectic, hateful, or even harmful to them or to someone they love? It staggers the mind. It makes no sense to our human brains. But quite frequently, God's better way for living contradicts what "makes sense" to us.

Revenge makes sense to our natural minds. If someone hurts us, we instinctively believe that the right thing to do is get even. (If you don't believe me, how did you feel the last time someone cut you off in traffic?) But as you may know, Jesus taught us the complete opposite. Revenge is only for God because revenge has a horrible habit of just creating more hatred and new desire for revenge.

So how can gratitude be a powerful tool in transforming our life despite the terrible things that are going on around us?

The Cases Are Real

One of my favorite TV shows of all time is *Judge Judy*. I was fascinated by how she managed her courtroom. It seemed like she was able to instantly sniff out any attempts at deception in the plaintiff's and defendant's stories, and I loved how she would openly confront them. She refused to put up with any nonsense. In fact, I found myself wishing that I could be that blunt with people all the time in my life. But I thank God that he gave me enough wisdom to remember that cutting people with words all the time is a recipe for a very lonely life.

Even though it was a TV show that had been edited by a crew of people to tell a story, the cases were real, the complaints in the briefs were real, and the plaintiff and defendant had experienced something that upset their world so much that they were willing to go to court to try to get some kind of justice.

I think that when we read the Bible, we should start off by reminding ourselves that the stories in it are of people who really walked this planet like you and me. Just like us, they experienced happiness and sorrow; they felt joy and pain; they experienced amazing victories and heart-wrenching defeats.

One such person in the Bible, whose story is filled with just about every human emotion you can think of, is Job.

Poor Job

Who was Job?

According to the Bible in the book of Job, we learn that he was a very good man. He reverenced God, shunned evil, and was blameless in the way he treated others. He was a family man, who had ten children and who loved his wife.

Through the wisdom that God had given him, he was also a successful businessman, who owned a lot of land and thousands upon thousands of heads of livestock.

In Job 1:3 (CEV), he is referred to as the "richest person in the east." He even regularly presented sacrifices to God as an act of intercession for his family.

Are you getting a pretty good picture of Job by now? Obviously, this is the type of guy who will always be successful and never experience any kind of trouble. Right?

Well, no.

You see, Satan knew of Job and Job's ways and was quite infuriated by his radiant testimony of goodness. It irked Satan to no end that this man continued to do good, despite the evil ways of the people all around him.

So, Satan did something rarely mentioned in the Bible. He traveled to the throne room of heaven and made an appearance before God! The nerve of this guy!

As he cringed away from God's power and glory, he complained to God that the only reason Job lived a righteous path was because of God's blessings. Satan even challenged that if God removed his blessings from Job, Job would turn on God and curse him.

Surprisingly, God agreed to the challenge. He had full confidence that Job's devotion to him wasn't based upon earthly riches, and God allowed Satan to tempt Job however he wanted except for one thing: Satan couldn't take Job's life.

The Devil, being a murderer, thief, and destroyer, immediately left heaven and traveled to Job's location to literally unleash hell upon Job's life.

Then It All Went Wrong

As Job stood examining part of his fields, he had no clue the terror that was about to befall him.

A messenger, bleeding and with torn clothes, came running up through the field. Out of breath, he warned Job, "We've been attacked! A raiding party has killed all of our ranchers and taken most of our livestock!"

Just as that servant fell on the ground from exhaustion, another messenger ran up from a different direction. With a look of horror on his face, he informed Job, "My lord, your livestock feeding in the far field have all been killed by a hail storm! I watched from under a rock. None survived!"

As the devastating news was just starting to sink into Job's mind, another servant ran up and knelt before Job. With tears running down his face, he sputtered out, "My master, your children were all feasting in your oldest son's house, when…a great windstorm came out of nowhere and collapsed the house on them…I don't know how to tell you this, but…your children are all dead."

Suddenly, the whole world seemed to spin. Job clutched onto his staff for balance. He shook his head in disbelief that any of this could have happened and especially not all at the same time! Somehow, he gathered enough strength to steady himself and proclaimed, "I came into this world with nothing, and I'll leave it with nothing. God has given and taken away, but God be praised!"

To me, Job's response is so astounding. In just the blink of an eye, he went from being the richest person in the region, to having practically nothing. It's like having saved your whole life for retirement, just to finally go to make a withdrawal and discover that someone else has completely wiped out your account, not even leaving a penny!

Job went from having a large family with children who loved him and got along very well with each other, to being childless. No longer would he hear their voices talking, laughing, and singing together, except in the echoes of his memories. Just a lonely silence filled the places they used to be.

I don't know about you, but if all of that happened to me in one day, I'd definitely say some things to God. I'd like to say what Job said, but to be real, I doubt those are the words that would come out of my mouth on such a day.

That makes me even more surprised when I read the last words of Job's response from Job 1:21 (NIV): "...may the name of the Lord be praised."

Wow. How can a person who has just experienced so much tragedy and turmoil all within the same day praise God?

I'll tell you how. Job lived a life of gratitude toward God.

Then Came the Boils

But this was just the beginning of Job's suffering and the trial of his faith in God. Soon, Job became very sick and broke out in sores all over his body. Not only did have to deal with the pain from the oozing sores, but he was hideous to look at.

At this point, Job's wife couldn't handle the stress any longer. They had lost most of what they owned, and her heart was absolutely broken from the death of her beloved children. Surely, she must've thought, "How could a righteous God allow a righteous man to suffer like this?"

She couldn't stand seeing her husband suffer any longer. She'd had all that she could take. Job 2:8-10 (NIV) records what happened next. Job's wife marched out to where Job had secluded himself, found him sitting in a pile of ashes, and demanded, "Are you still holding on to your integrity?!"

He probably looked up at her, startled by the sudden outburst.

When he didn't respond, she begged, "Curse God and die!"

It's like she was saying, "God has turned his back on you and taken everything from you. Give God the finger, so that he'll finish you off and end your suffering. I can't take watching you be tortured like this."

I wonder if you've ever felt like Job or Job's wife in your life.

Job shook his head and replied to his wife, "You are talking like a foolish woman. Shall we accept good from God, and not trouble?"

I find the last sentence fascinating. He refused to question God's actions. Even if God was the one responsible for committing the terrible things to him, Job was so rock-solidly steadfast in his devotion to God that he humbled himself before God and refused to sin against God, despite all of the suffering that came his way.

Job chose to be grateful toward God for anything and everything, and this gave him the hope and power to look for a new day of blessing in God. Listen to Job's confession of faith from Job 19:25-27 (NIV):

> "I know that my redeemer lives, and that in the end he will stand on the earth. And after my skin has been destroyed, yet in my flesh, I will see God; I myself will see him with my own eyes—I, and not another. How my heart yearns within me!"

In the midst of his storm, Job's heart longed to be with God. Furthermore, Job has faith that one day, he will be redeemed from his suffering and will even see God!

Many Bible commentators, including early church writers, believe that those three verses are prophetically referring to the coming of the ultimate Redeemer, Jesus Christ. And one day, there will be a resurrection of the dead, and we will appear before God.

My mind is blown away by the idea that out of Job's suffering, a prophecy about the hope of resurrection from a Redeemer—who suffered centuries later on a cross for our salvation—would be given to the world! Even though it may have seemed like God had abandoned Job, he was there with him all the time and even blessed him with a vision of the Messiah.

I Don't Feel So Good...

As I was writing this chapter, I started running a fever and had chills. I went to the doctor, thinking it was a sinus infection, but learned that I had contracted Covid-19. I was shocked. I had been social distancing, wearing a mask, and religiously washing my hands. But now, I was infected!

I felt tense. That week, three pastors in my area had died, two from Covid and one never woke up from his sleep. Covid was spreading all throughout the community, and each day, the news was filled with rising numbers of new infections and Covid-related deaths. I wondered to myself, "Will I be the next one to pass?"

I started feeling worse and wrapped myself up in a blanket to stay warm when I heard these words from my wife, Rhonda: "Jeff, I don't feel so good."

Oh boy, now I was really concerned. I love Rhonda dearly, and now, she was sick, too.

Together we endured days of the Covid symptoms–body aches, fever, chills, headaches, sore throat, and exhaustion. I wish I could tell you that when this sickness started, my mind stayed positive and grateful, but it did not. I was hearing about so much death, fear for Rhonda and I crept into my heart and mind.

But somewhere in the middle of my sickness, my mind went back to Job's words:

"Shall I only accept the good from God?"

I don't believe that God gave me Covid, but I do believe that he can take the bad things that happen to us and turn them around into something good. Rhonda and I recovered completely, and our recovery is a testimony to the power of God. And experiencing pain while I was writing about Job really helped connect me better to the power of his story.

Being on an Airplane

How about you? Are you living in thanks despite what might be going on in your life right now? If you're not, remember Job. In the middle of all his problems and pain, he declared God to be his Redeemer.

Your mind might be overwhelmed right now with, "How am I going to get through this?"

I'd like you to imagine yourself on an airplane. You're sitting in your seat with your seatbelt on, looking out the window at the wing. Suddenly the engines roar to life, and you feel yourself pushed back into your seat.

Like a lot of people, you feel your heartbeat quicken as the ride gets bumpier and bumpier. You may even think, "I want off this thing!" But it's too late. The journey has already started, and you're strapped in for the ride.

And then, you feel the nose of the plane rising higher. There are some sounds and bumps, and before you know it, the plane is completely in the air! In just a few minutes, you look out the window and can already see the tops of the clouds. In just a little more time, the pilot comes on over the intercom and announces that you're at cruising altitude, and you're free to move around the cabin.

Now think about the fuel tanks in the plane. You didn't see anyone fuel the plane, but you know that it's there because the plane is pushing forward at high speed despite the winds pushing against it.

Gratitude in your life is like the fuel in the plane. When you are facing adversity, gratitude fuels you along to a steadfast peace in God no matter what winds rage against you.

Will you be a person whose plane is grounded at the airport, stuck in the doldrums of life, or will you take the opportunity to build up your gratitude to soar in the peace of full cruising altitude?

The choice is yours. I encourage you to continue reading forward in this book to learn specific ways to develop a thanks-living mindset.

Chapter 2

Grateful That God Is for Me

from Chesnee

As a young adult, I watched parents interacting with their children, and I'd think, "Why did they do that? I could do a better job than them." Of course, that was before I had a child of my own to raise. Since then, I have reversed my position and stand before you now, proclaiming: Parenting is hard!

One of the quick wake-up calls I received as a parent is that simple things with kids can be so difficult. When I was a child and my parents said things like, "Brush your teeth, take a bath, do your homework," I'd get irritated and sometimes refuse to do what they ordered. I'd think, "Why do I need to brush my teeth? I just did it yesterday!"

Now that my perspective has changed, I understand that my parents were just taking care of me. But most kids don't get this. They don't get why they have to eat their vegetables, why they shouldn't just run out into the street, and why they shouldn't jump off the roof even if they're wearing a towel as a cape.

And it continues throughout the teen years, too. Sometimes, they don't understand why they shouldn't speed when they drive, why they shouldn't hang out with a person, why they shouldn't skip school, and why they shouldn't drink or do drugs.

As a parent, sometimes I want to shout: "Don't you know I'm just trying to protect you! I'm not the enemy here; I am FOR you!"

I think that God does the same for us. I believe that God is like the ultimate parent and that he is FOR our good. And, just like a parent, I think he is saying to all of us, "Stop fighting against me! I love you and want what's best for you."

Discontent

God was the first "parent," and he had two children, who were obedient for a while but eventually rebelled against God's authority. I don't think that Adam and Eve understood that God was trying to protect them from a future dominated by death, pain, and strenuous work.

But even though our great, great, great (and so on) grandparents lived in beautiful perfection, had daily visits with God face-to-face, and lacked for nothing, they eventually weren't content with all of that. They wanted more. And when they were enticed with something new, BOOM, they took it and rebelled.

All of these millennia later, I can sit here in judgment over Adam and Eve and think I would've done a better job–kind of like I did earlier with parents before I had a child–but in reality, I think I would've made the same mistake they made.

Why? Well, it seems to be in our human nature to want what we can't or shouldn't have. Daily, we have a battle that takes place in our minds between being content with what we have or being discontent, and this battle of thoughts can take place in just about any area of our lives.

When we become restless and impatient, we forget that God is working out a plan for us, and we can become downright ungrateful toward him.

Our enemy, Satan, wants nothing more than to thwart God's plans for our life. And one of Satan's classic tricks is to tempt people with a shortcut to get what they want. Sadly, Satan's tempting shortcuts bring pain, disillusionment, and emptiness. Instead of receiving what God would like to bless us with, we receive a disappointing counterfeit of the real deal.

And that's what happened to Adam and Eve in the garden. They ate the forbidden fruit, and, instead of becoming gods, they became mortals. Furthermore, God kicked them out of the beautiful garden he made for them, and they'd have to work and suffer to survive in a harsh world.

In a way, they got ahead of God's plan, thinking that they knew better than him. And we can easily do the same thing in our lives. Living in grateful contentment helps keep us away from temptation and settles our hearts so that we can better hear God's leading by his Spirit each day.

The Apostle Paul gives us a reality check in 1 Corinthians 4:7-8 about contentment and gratitude:

> Isn't everything you have and everything you are sheer gifts from God? So what's the point of all this comparing and competing? You already have all you need. (MSG)

If we are going to trust that God is for us, then we have to learn to be content with what he has given us. But how do we do that?

Rick Warren, the author of *The Purpose Driven Life*, says that envy is looking at others and saying, "Why them?" and then becoming resentful. Contentment looks inward and says, "God, why me? Why did you choose to bless me with what I really don't deserve?"

Overcoming Discontent

So how can we move ourselves away from being envious of what others have and being resentful about our own situation?

Let me share with you a few solutions that have helped me tremendously in my life.

1. Stop comparing yourself to others

Comparison is tricky and can easily sneak up on us. We see that a co-worker got a new car, while we're still driving one from years back. Something in our brain dings, and we may say how happy we are for them, but many times, we would rather be the one driving the new car.

We're scrolling through social media and see tons of pictures of a friend on an expensive vacation at a tropical beach with palm trees and crystal blue water, and we think with a frown, "Must be nice," as we look outside at a cold dreary winter scene.

The popular kids at school show up dressed in the latest trend–it's like they wear new clothes every day! Or they're amazing in all of their classes. Or they're the all-star athlete who always wins the game for the team.

It can be so easy to fall into the comparison trap anywhere and everywhere.

So how do we fight it?

First, you have to recognize when you're falling into the comparison trap. As soon as you realize that you're comparing yourself to someone else or to someone else's possessions or to someone else's life, call it out in your mind! Literally tell yourself, "I'm falling into the comparison trap, and I'm stopping this right now."

Second, stop and shift your focus on what God has done for you. Mentally, start listing out ways that God has blessed you. If you're a Christian, God has blessed you with salvation and the hope of eternal life in heaven, which are the most valuable gifts in the universe!

And God has blessed you with many, many more things. If you're reading this right now, he's blessed you with life, the ability to breathe on your own, your heart is beating, and so on.

Don't become a victim of the comparison trap! Take control of your thinking and see how richly blessed you are!

2. Happiness is all about your attitude

I confess that this solution to overcoming discontent is tough for me. Full disclosure, I'm a glass-half-empty kind of person naturally. I wasn't born with innate optimism. I'm careful, cautious, analytical–which can sometimes lead me to be cynical.

The only way that I can combat this is to give thanks to God. I say out loud or in my mind, "Thank you, God, that you're doing this in my life, and thank you that you will take care of that." It is faith and gratefulness combined.

3. Silence fear with faith

Fear can steal gratitude right out of your mind. I know this firsthand. I like to have a lot of my questions answered upfront, and I definitely want a plan in place before I take any steps. These things help me feel calm and ready to tackle a project at home and work. Of course, life rarely gives you all this stuff upfront.

Maybe like you, I frequently find life coming at me from many directions, and before I've had a chance to process everything, it's like more rushes in. When this happens, my natural inclination is to feel overwhelmed, tense, and fearful.

During these moments, I have to stop and remind myself of what Romans 8:31 says:

> What then shall we say to these things? If God is for us, who can be against us? (NKJV)

Wow, *if God is for us.* If you are a follower of Jesus, God is for you! Think about how amazing that is. Who can defeat God? No one! Who can win against God? No one!

This doesn't mean that we won't experience times of discouragement and disappointment. It means that *despite* those things, God is ultimately working out something good in our lives. And by faith, we can stand strong on God's Word and on the truth that God always keeps his promises.

What about the fear of not having enough? This one attacks my mind a lot. You may also have negative thoughts like these pop up out of nowhere: "What if I don't have enough time? What if I don't have enough energy? What if I run out of money? What if this all goes horribly wrong?"

When I find myself thinking thoughts like these, I run to the hope-filling promise of Philippians 4:19, which says:

> And my God shall supply all your need according to his riches in glory by Christ Jesus. (NKJV)

God already has all that we will ever need. He has already overcome, and he's already answered. You may have to wait, but he has already provided for what you truly need. So you can give thanks to God now while you wait.

Overcoming Fear

Speaking of fear, we all encounter it in various ways all throughout our lives. If we're not careful, it can even dominate our lives. I'm writing this during the Covid-19 pandemic, and it feels like the whole world is more fearful and tense than any other time in my life.

With every day filled with seemingly worse news and endless uncertainties about what is coming next, I have had to practice two very important concepts to disarm fear and boost my gratitude.

1. **When I focus more on God than on my problem, it changes my perspective**

At Stockbridge Community Church, we've said many times, "Remind your problem how big your God is rather than telling God how big your problem is."

It's natural to focus on the problem; that's how the problem-solving sections of our brain work. Our mind focuses on problems so that it can start figuring out solutions to them. The problem becomes when we spend so much time thinking about something that our minds inflate it into a giant that we can't conquer.

When we focus more on God, we start to reflect on how God is actually far larger and far more powerful than any problem that can challenge us. By focusing on God and giving him praise for bringing us through whatever we're facing, suddenly those problems, which looked impossible to scale, shrink!

Like Max Lucado says, "Our anxiety decreases as my understanding of God increases."

2. Repeat what is true

No matter how true our fears may seem to us, fear is usually a lie, misunderstanding, or exaggeration with a lot of imagination dressing it up. Some fears obviously have merit: a bear charging at you with teeth flared has merit! But if we're not careful, our minds can turn just about any situation into a bear running at us with teeth flared if we spend days dwelling on it.

It's sad that so many people take the joy out of their lives by wasting their days worrying about stuff that most likely won't even happen. I heard one time that 95% of the stuff that we worry about doesn't ever happen.

Now, everyone's life is different, but I can attest to the fact that most of the things I've worried about in my life have never happened. So, when we have fearful thoughts rising up inside us, we need to examine the fear, pick out the lie or exaggeration, and replace it with what is true.

You may ask, "What is true?" My answer is the Bible, God's Word. It is filled with promises that you can challenge your fears with. Here are some of my favorites to combat fear:

> It is the Lord who goes before you. He will be with you; he will not leave you or forsake you. Do not fear or be dismayed. -Deuteronomy 31:8 (ESV)

> My flesh and my heart may fail, but God is the strength of my heart and my portion forever. -Psalm 73:26 (ESV)

> Peace I leave with you; my peace I give you. I do not give to you as the world gives. Do not let your hearts be troubled and do not be afraid. -John 14:27 (NIV)

God is for us! Learning to be content can keep the practice of gratitude in our lives. Overcoming our fears by replacing them with God's truth can also make thankfulness more of a reality. Remember that God's words aren't just words to make us feel good; they are life changing and powerful! His Word is alive, active, and transformative!

Before School Begins

Every year, before school begins, we have a prayer over the children and students of our church. We bring all of the kids into "big church," and we have a tradition of picking a song to sing over them after the congregation prays over them.

In 2020, there was no better song than Kari Jobe's "The Blessing." My favorite part of the song is the bridge, which repeats the words, "He is for you!" That year, I was filled with joy as I looked out across the kids filling the altar area. They were singing along with the song, "He is for you, he is for you!"

I thought, of all the ideas that get planted in their minds, here is something that they can hold onto forever. God is for us; why should we be afraid?

This I know, that God is for me. -Psalm 56:9 (ESV)

Chapter 3

Gratitude: The Stress Reliever

from Jeff

Raise your hand if you've felt stressed within the last year. I don't know if your hand is raised, but mine sure is! If you've experienced pressure-cooker-like stress over the past year, you're not alone.

Over the past couple of years, we've experienced stress in just about every area of our lives. Sickness, economic downturn, racial division, political tension, shortages, inflation, and death of friends and family members have all confronted us in a magnitude unimaginable just a few years ago.

But even before 2020, people's lives were filled with stress. Whether it's related to work, relationships, health, and finances, the average person, any place in the world, has some degree of stress.

To See a Mouse

Walt Disney World is advertised as the happiest place on earth; surely there couldn't be any stress there.

Rhonda and our kids love Disney, so we've taken several trips to Disney World in Orlando throughout the years. We've had a lot of fun, but I can't say the trips were "stress-free." Picture this.

You and your family got up extra early at your hotel so that you could get to the park before the big crowds get there. But now it's midday, and you're feeling very hungry and tired. Your feet are already hurting from walking and standing in line so much, and the pathways are now crammed with people. The summer sun is bearing down on you with no relief anywhere.

One of your children has exploded into a full-blown tantrum because the attraction they wanted to ride is closed. The other child is about to burst into tears because the ice cream–which you just spent an arm and a leg for–has fallen onto the street and is now oozing every-where. As one of your children demands, "I WANT TO EAT," you look at the long lines of people snaking around the closest food stalls and groan.

Before you can even decide which way to walk, a clap of thunder, followed by a sudden downpour, sends the crowd scurrying in a panic for the closest covering.

"The happiest place on earth?" you think, shaking your head.

Now, I know this example is a little extreme, but I also know that a lot of people have had similar experiences on family trips, because they've told me so.

In some ways, stress is unavoidable. It can confront us at school, at home, at work, in public, wherever we are.

Jesus was well acquainted with stress. At the time that he lived, ten-sions between the Jews and the occupying Romans were boiling over. Jewish Zealots attacked and murdered Roman soldiers in the market-place. Roman soldiers brutally crucified anyone who they believed was a criminal or Zealot. Taxes were high, average lifespans were short, and food was scarce. Talk about stress!

Yet, Jesus pointed to a different way of thinking and living than what his neighbors engaged in. Listen to his words from John 16:33:

"I have told you these things, so that in me you may have peace. In this world you will have trouble. But take heart! I have overcome the world." (NIV)

Wow. The same issue with stress that those ancient people faced is the same for us today. It's not how to completely eliminate stress. Jesus confirms that there will always be trouble in this world. We can't completely get rid of stress.

Instead, our hope is in how to manage stress with God's help, so that it passes around us but does not drown us.

The Big 5

Where we experience stress can be divided into five categories: physical health, mental health, emotional health, relational health, and spiritual health. Let's take a look at each of them to get a better picture of what is going on.

Our Physical Health

Many physical problems can result from or be made worse by stress. High blood pressure can be related to the way that people react to stress. Living and working in a high stress environment can be a strong precursor to a heart attack. It can rob you of restful sleep and rush how quickly you age. And stress can even make joint and back pain worse.

Our Mental Health

Multiple types of mental hindrances and disorders can be connected to stress or worsened by it. Countless studies have shown that people in general function worse as the level of stress increases. Our ability to think clearly and make good decisions can be greatly affected by chronic stress. My guess is that if you think back over your life and look at the ten worst decisions you've made, six of those moments were connected to poor decisions you made while being stressed out.

Our Emotional Health

Living under a load of stress can make us irritable, snappy, unfriendly, angry, and vengeful. In fact, I bet that someone just came to your mind as you read the previous sentence. Is that person's life like a constant whirlwind of emotion and drama? (Now, don't be mad at me, but if no one came to your mind, you might be that person.)

Our Relational Health

When we have no *margin* in our lives–extra space and time to be able to interact calmly with people–we may easily fall into being irritable with coworkers, family, and friends. Instead of turning to our closest relationships as safe havens, we can take out our stressed-out frustrations on the very people we love. We must all find a better way of dealing with stress than that!

Our Spiritual Health

Have you ever noticed that when we have a lot of things to do, one of the first things to get discarded can be our prayer time and our Bible reading time? This is the very reason that I intentionally start my day with Bible reading and prayer because I know that if I try to put them off till later, they'll get lost in my busy day, and I won't do them. We have to feed our spiritual person just like we have to feed our physical body, or our spiritual health will decline to the point that we're "running on empty." Let me share with you this powerful truth: You may be physically exhausted, but if you're spiritually prayed up and strong, you will be able to handle almost any stress that is thrown at you.

Whoa.

I don't know about you, but the information in those five categories is some heavy stuff! So, let's take a deep breath, hold it, and release it. And let's now look to the hope of a better way of living.

Jail Hope

If you've flipped through or read the New Testament, you've probably run across the book of *Philippians*. What many people don't know about this letter to the Christians in the city of Philippi is that it was written by the Apostle Paul while he was in jail for preaching about Jesus. You'd think that Paul would sound depressed or angry in this letter, since he had been wrongfully imprisoned, but the opposite is true.

Philippians is filled with joy and rejoicing. But how? Paul was under constant watch by a Roman guard, and if Paul's friends weren't able to bring him food, he didn't eat since the prison refused to feed him.

How can someone who is innocent be treated so terribly and unfairly and yet find joy?

When I was on a mission trip to Honduras, our group visited a jail that had similar conditions to what Paul would've experienced in his time. As the security guards opened the doors and our small ministry team entered, I was shocked by the grim conditions that these prisoners lived in. Each cell was just a tiny cement block room with a small, bar-covered window. There was no heating or air conditioning in the building; everyone endured the cold of the winter and the unrelenting heat of the long summer. The smell of body odor and human waste was overpowering!

As our mission group walked along the main corridor and passed out food to each prisoner, I could see the intense desperation and gratitude in each of their eyes as each person took the food and began to eat. Afterward, I asked the missionary leading our team why we had taken them food. He gave a sad shake of his head and said, "If no one brings them food; they won't have anything to eat; the jails don't feed them."

These were the same dreadful conditions that Paul found himself trapped in. Yet, he wrote these words in Philippians 4:4:

Rejoice in the Lord always. I will say it again: Rejoice! (NIV)

Wow! What a game-changing outlook!

I've imagined myself sitting in a prison cell in the same conditions that Paul suffered through and asked myself if I would have Paul's same extraordinary outlook. And I've got to confess; it would be a struggle for me to keep a positive attitude, especially being ill-treated and having my freedom taken away. But eventually, my mind would remember that God is with me wherever I am, whatever I go through, and that truth brings *hope* and gives us a reason to *rejoice*.

Christmas Rejoicing

Let me share with you a little moment from my life when I witnessed rejoicing.

Christmas was quickly approaching, and my daughter, Katelyn, wanted a new smartphone. She had been using an old flip phone for a while. All of her friends had already upgraded to smartphones a couple of years before.

Now, so that you understand how I do Christmas at the Daws household, I always get my wife and children a gift specifically from me. They get other presents from Rhonda and me together or just Rhonda, but I always look for something that I can present to each of them.

The catch is that it's not necessarily what they've asked for. A lot of times, I get them something practical that I think will benefit their life. So needless to say, my kids aren't always thrilled with my "special" Christmas present.

So, on this particular Christmas, Katelyn had already opened other presents and seemed to be having a good time. And then I said with excitement in my voice as I pointed, "Hey, Katelyn, open *that* present; *that* one right over there."

She looked at the rather plain looking box and rolled her eyes as she stated, "Oh boy, it's one of Dad's presents."

I thought to myself, "Baby girl, you better believe it's one of my presents; just you wait and see!"

In no rush, Katelyn retrieved the box from under the tree and smirked as she thought about how she would return whatever it was I'd gotten her.

As she tore off the paper and opened the box, her face suddenly lit up in complete astonishment. Inside was a brand new, shiny smartphone. Tears of joy started running down her face as she lifted the phone out of the box. She was so happy that, for a moment, she didn't even know what to say! She ran over and gave me a big hug and thanked me over and over.

Katelyn's reaction has become how I picture rejoicing. Life's challenges and daily stress may try to bring me down, or I might feel like I'm just "getting through." But when I refocus my mind on the wonderful truth that God has already given me the greatest gift of salvation through Jesus Christ and the hope of Heaven, I can't help but do as Paul said and rejoice in the Lord!

Replace Anxious Thoughts

While being forced to live in a disgusting prison, the Apostle Paul had to have faced anxious thoughts. Darkness, sudden loud noises, rude taunting from the guards, uncertainty whether anyone would bring him food, and the screams and cries of prisoners had to be unnerving to

Paul at times. And yet, in Philippians 4:6, Paul challenges the horrors around him by saying:

> Do not be anxious about anything, but in everything,
> by prayer and petition, with thanksgiving, present your
> requests to God. (NIV)

The Greek word translated as *anxious* in this verse means to be *pulled in many directions*. If that's not a definition for modern life, I don't know what is!

With constant notifications on our phones and computers, news 24/7, long work hours and side jobs, after school activities for kids multiple days of the week, sickness, relationships, and on, and on, we are pulled in so many directions! And all of this constant rush, constant pressure, constant stress, and no time to rest can trigger anxiety in any of us.

But Paul gives us a cure for much of this anxiety through the verse above. By releasing our worries and concerns to God through prayer and by giving thanks for what God has already done in our lives and will do, we can literally feel anxiety leaving our body.

Another verse that connects with this de-stressing through speaking thanks to God is Proverbs 18:21, which reveals:

> The tongue has the power of life and death. (NIV)

Literally, our words have the power to encourage and strengthen us or the power to discourage and weaken us. By speaking praises and thanks to God out loud, we are saying by faith, "God, I believe that you've got this, and I know that you have the power to turn everything around for the good."

The next time that you are feeling stressed out or anxious about something, I challenge you to stop, take a deep breath, ask God to help with the situation, and give thanks to him for turning the situation around.

Tightwire Act

Nik Wallenda's family wasn't quite like everyone else's. They performed acrobatics, stunts, and many other death-defying acts that, if we had to do them, would send most of us into an all-out panic attack!

But at a young age, Nik learned to walk on a wire. At first, the wire was very low to the ground, but as he grew in confidence and skill, the wire was raised higher and higher. Throughout his life, he continued taking on tougher challenges, always pushing himself to go higher.

Then, on June 15, 2012, Nik confronted his greatest and riskiest challenge when he looked out at a narrow wire, 1,800 feet long, suspended over Niagara Falls! If he fell, no nets would save him from the rocks and raging water below. At this height, hitting water would smash his body like hitting concrete, and even if he survived the impact, the powerful currents would pull him down to a watery grave.

This insane high wire attempt had attracted much attention, and TV crews were there to broadcast the whole event live. I don't know why someone would perform such a daring stunt, but I have a good idea of what kept Nik calm inside as he readied to step out onto a shaking wire high in the air.

Isaiah 26:3 says:

> You will keep in perfect peace all who trust in you, all whose thoughts are fixed on you. (NLT)

As Rhonda and I watched the event live on TV, we both held our breath as Nik started his record-breaking walk. From far away, it looked like the wire was perfectly still as Nik carefully pushed forward, but when the camera shot showed a close up, we could see the wire vibrating and moving in the wind!

We sat on the edge of our seats, amazed at what we were seeing and what we were hearing. You see, Nik wore a microphone that was broadcasting his words as he walked. You might think that he'd remain silent as he concentrated or that he'd curse when he started to feel his foot slip. But for the whole journey, Nik prayed out loud!

Between his heavy breaths and the whistling of the wind, he'd say, "Thank you, Jesus. Thank you for your presence. Thank you for the strength to continue on."

I don't know which I found more amazing: his sheer courage to walk the high wire or his unwavering faith in God.

Now, chances are extremely high that neither you nor I will ever do a high wire act, but we all experience walking through unknown territory in our lives, and it can be just as terrifying as having to walk over Niagara Falls. When we go through these moments, we should do just like Nik Wallenda did: replace our anxious thoughts with words of prayer and thanksgiving to God.

Stop the Stinking Thinking

Every couple of years, I re-read a book that had a powerful impact on my life. I first encountered it when I was a young preacher and was seeking to find who I was as a leader. As I read through Zig Ziglar's book *See You at the Top*, I was challenged over and over with ideas and concepts that were revolutionary to me. Ziglar's easy writing style, motivation, and catchphrases stuck with me and launched me into thinking differently about my life.

"We need a checkup from the neck up," and, "stinking thinking," Ziglar coined in reference to defeatist attitudes. As I continued reading through his book, I started examining my own thoughts throughout the day, and I was shocked by what I found!

Negative thoughts, critical judgments, and complaining dominated a whole lot more of my thinking than I would've liked to admit. But you can't change and get better until you admit to yourself what's holding you back.

I had to change my thinking during the day, but how?

So I went to the book that has changed my life more than any other book: the Bible. And sure enough, Philippians 4:8 gives the solution to overcoming negative and stressful thoughts that rise up throughout any day:

> …whatever is true, whatever is noble, whatever is right, whatever is pure, whatever is lovely, whatever is admirable–if anything is excellent or praiseworthy–think about such things.

Instead of leaving your mind in "autopilot" mode, where you just let your thoughts run wild with whatever springs up in it during your day, I challenge you to take control over your mind when you notice stressful, anxious, and negative thoughts popping up.

Instead of focusing on something that is stressing you out, take a moment to focus on something that is true or noble or right. Spend a moment thinking about something that is pure or lovely or admirable.

There are many short but powerful Bible passages that you could memorize to say and reflect on to counter stress, fear, and anxiety. Two of my favorites are the Lord's Prayer, found in Matthew 6:9-13, and Psalm 23, the Shepherd's Psalm. Both of these passages have brought me peace during trying and stressful times more times than I can count!

The Disappearing Red

To give you another way of thinking about changing your thinking, I'd like you to picture a clear jar filled with water. You can see straight through it to the other side. Now, I'd like you to visualize picking up a small container of red food coloring and adding the food coloring to the clean water.

The smoky wisps of red dye curl and fall to the bottom of the jar before expanding outward and eventually filling the entire jar with a reddish cloud. The red dye represents stressful thoughts, and the red cloud symbolizes a person who is completely stressed out!

So how could we reverse the process and help this jar return to its peaceful, clear state?

You might say, "Just take it to a sink and dump it out and refill it."

That's a great idea, but if the jar symbolizes our mind, we can never fully empty our mind of thoughts. If you don't believe me, try to think of nothing for the next five minutes. Of course, you won't even need five minutes before you're already thinking about something that needs to be done immediately, what you're having for your next meal, what time you have to pick up the kids, whether you paid a bill, and so on.

So if we can't empty the jar, how can we get rid of the red dye of stressing thoughts?

For the answer, imagine once again the jar filled with red water. Now see yourself picking up a large pitcher filled with clear water. Begin pouring the water from the pitcher into the jar. Red water from the jar immediately starts to run over the lid and down the glass. Don't worry about the floor because a wide pan underneath the jar is collecting all the runoff.

As you continue pouring water from the pitcher, something magical happens: the deep red color of the water in the jar fades to light red and then lighter red until finally, every last trace of red has disappeared from the jar!

My friend, this simple demonstration shows how we can dilute and replace stressful thoughts we are experiencing by "pouring in" good and peaceful thoughts. Specifically, reading verses from the Bible is a powerful way to "clean" our minds of negative and anxious thoughts. Saying gratitude-filled thanks to God and singing praises to him are two more ways we can flood our minds with the stress-cleansing power of the Holy Spirit.

So from this day forward, whenever you find yourself filled with troubling thoughts, remember the picture of the pitcher pouring clean water into the jar of red-dyed water, and you'll remember what you need to do to flush out your mind.

Chapter 4

Grateful That God Is with Me

from Chesnee

I love Thanksgiving. It's a low-key holiday for me. I'm not required to decorate or buy presents for everyone in the family. My only responsibility is to find a really good Honey Baked Ham coupon, put in my order, and let those brilliant chefs at Honey Baked Ham prepare a delicious ham dripping with their world-famous sweet, golden glaze. Yum!

In Georgia, it's also a good weather time of the year–not too cold (hopefully) or too hot. It's also usually the weekend that the Georgia Bulldogs play the Georgia Tech Yellow Jackets, and, my apologies to you if you're a Tech fan, the Dawgs usually win.

It's Finally Here!

As the Thanksgiving of 2020 approached, I was really excited about getting to see my family face-to-face again. We were finally out of the lock-down phase of the Covid pandemic, and I couldn't wait to be with my mom, dad, and grandmother.

Before we left to go out of town, I decided to visit the doctor about some minor symptoms I'd been having. The doctor tested me, and after the examination, proclaimed that I just had a infection. He prescribed some antibiotics and sent me on my way.

I was so happy. All I had to do was take three days of medication, and I would feel great.

I took my regimen for the day before we were to leave. After packing the car, my husband Danny, my son Drew, and I took off for my parents' house in Toccoa. And when we arrived, it was so wonderful to see my parents' smiling faces at the front door! After almost a year of being separated, it felt so good to hug them.

All was so good…until I woke up the next morning.

I almost jumped out of bed from sudden sharp pains in my legs and arms. I had no clue as to what was happening, and I worried. I'd never experienced anything quite like these sensations before. I'd feel a stab that was then followed by numbness all over.

Danny was greatly concerned, too, and recommended that I call the doctor immediately, which I did. I was hoping the doctor would have some kind of comforting words for me to alleviate my fears, but he just plainly told me that the medication I'd taken *could* cause side effects like I was experiencing.

"*Could* cause…" the words echoed in my mind.

With Thanksgiving just moments away, this was not what I wanted to hear.

The day went on, and despite my family's prayers for me and my own cries to God for help, my symptoms worsened. I ended up spending the week on my mom's couch, barely able to eat, riddled with anxiety, nausea, and pain, and now very afraid for what this meant for my future.

I started googling what other people had been through when they had bad reactions to this drug, and as you can guess, their nightmare experiences sent me spiraling down a hole of hopelessness.

Thoughts like, "What will my future look like as a mother and wife who can't lift anything in her arms?" and "How can I work if I can't even type on a computer?" troubled my mind even further. My family treated me with such love, but in that moment, all I could see was my pain and what I had lost.

Pastor Jeff and Rhonda called me a couple of times to check on me and pray with me over the phone. I've known them for most of my life, and they have meant so much to me for so long. I greatly appreciated their calls and prayers.

But above all, Pastor Jeff said something to me, so simple but so profound, that it ended up becoming my rallying cry. He confidently said, "This is going to pass." When the bouts of pain and anxiety overtook me again and again, literally shaking my whole body, I would encourage myself with, "This IS going to pass."

Over the next months, I underwent multiple tests to investigate possible neurological damage. And I thank God that nothing more serious was found. Slowly over time, the odd stabbing pains and numbness have lessened to the point that I am able to function pretty close to how I did before the bad reaction to the medication.

One thing I know for certain from the very start to where I am today is that God has been with me throughout the whole ordeal. When I started to feel like I was alone or had been abandoned, he let me know that he was still with me and that he had not abandoned me. And if God is with me, then I must let thankfulness and gratefulness be my guides. Just like 1 Thessalonians 5:18 says:

> Give thanks in all circumstances, for this is God's will for you in Christ Jesus. (NIV)

How can we give thanks to God in every circumstance?

Radical Gratitude

The Greek word translated into English as "in all" circumstances in the previous verse is *pos*, which can mean *any, all, everything, all the time, anywhere and everywhere, the whole thing*. With that knowledge, we could expand the meaning of 1 Thessalonians 5:18 to:

> Give thanks in all and in any circumstances, in every-thing, all the time, anywhere and everywhere, for the whole thing, for this is God's will for you in Christ Jesus.

Wow. Starting to get the picture of what God is saying to us in this verse?

I've had many people come to me throughout the years and ask, "How do I find the will of God in my life?" They'll ask me, "How do I know who to marry? What job should I take? What college major should I select?"

These are all important questions to consider, but before recommending anything else, I redirect them to God. And let me say that if it's important enough for you to worry about or to take time deciding, it's important enough to pray about and to give thanks about!

You might say, "How can I give thanks? Nothing's happened yet?" or "I've already made a decision, and it's not going well." To these questions, I say again, "Give thanks!" Thank God ahead of time for answering your prayers. If your circumstances are not good, again, thank God that he is with you and will bring you through the challenge.

Right now, take a moment just to pause and confess, "God, thank you that even though _____ (fill in the blank), I know that you are with me and are helping me grow into a better and stronger person."

Wisdom from the Psalmist

The Psalmist David wrote in Psalm 23:4:

> Even though I walk through the darkest valley, I will
> fear no evil… (NIV)

That "even though" in this verse is such a significant phrase. He's not talking about a basic level of gratitude. This is graduate level gratitude. David is proclaiming, "Even though I'm terrified by the circumstances, even though I don't feel strong enough to make it through this valley, even though I feel like I'm alone right now, I know, that I know, that I know, that you are with me God and that I will make it through this valley! When I'm weak, you make me strong! And I will put all of my faith and hope in you!"

And God isn't just with us as we travel to our destination of a new job or healing or financial stability. He is with us for the complete journey of our life.

David was an outdoorsman. He grew up as a shepherd tending his father's sheep. As a man, he hid in caves and the mountains to escape from the fury of King Saul. As a writer, he frequently incorporated scenes from nature into his psalms. Psalm 121:1-2 is an example:

> I look up to the mountains–does my help come from
> there? My help comes from the Lord who made heaven
> and earth. (NLT)

Imagine young David walking along a hot, stony path. His pace is slow now. Earlier, he had to chase down some sheep that had escaped from the fold and is now carrying one with a wounded leg. He's tired, but he keeps going because he knows that if he's in the wilderness for too long, he could be attacked by a wild animal.

A cool breeze brushes by, and he pauses a moment to take a deep breath. As he does so, he lets his eyes drift up to the tops of the mountains in front of him. They look like towering giants in the late afternoon light, but he shakes his head.

"My help isn't coming from the mountains. My help is coming from the Lord God who made the mountains."

I know that God is ultimately in control of my life. I know that God can create good even from a rotten situation. And I know that God can even turn stupid mistakes that we make around for a better tomorrow for us. I know that no matter what happens, God isn't going to stop loving us.

You Don't Even Smell Like Smoke!

In the book of Daniel, there is a powerful account of what God can do for the people who worship and give praise to him.

Three young Hebrew men, named Shadrach, Meshach, and Abednego, had been taken captive with thousands of other Jews after the Babylonian army conquered ancient Israel. They were forced to leave their homeland and live in ancient Babylon.

There, these three were found to be quite intelligent and were given a fast-tracked education in the ways of the Babylonians. In addition to learning about literature, mathematics, and customs, they were also forced to learn about Babylon's religion, which featured several gods and even elevated the king to a "son" of one of the gods.

Now, Shadrach, Meshach, and Abednego were steadfast in their devotion to the One True God of Israel and refused to bow to or worship any idol or any other god. This unwavering loyalty to God would soon be tested beyond anything that we can imagine.

Craving the worship of his people, King Nebuchadnezzar of Babylon commissioned the building of a towering, gold-covered statue of himself. Once it was built, he made it mandatory for everyone to bow down to it and worship it when trumpets sounded. Anyone who refused would be executed by being thrown into a blazing furnace!

Upon hearing of the king's edict, Shadrach, Meshach, and Abednego decided that they would continue to worship only the One True God and put their faith in him. And when the trumpets blew, everyone in the crowd bowed to the ground and worshiped the statue…except for Shadrach, Meshach, and Abednego.

As King Nebuchadnezzar looked out across the plain at the crowd of loyal subjects, he probably smiled in delight at receiving the people's worship. But then his eyes caught sight of three people still standing. The king was enraged by their disobedience and had his guards snatch them out of the crowd for questioning.

But, when the king recognized Shadrach, Meshach, and Abednego, he paused. In the process of becoming residents of Babylon, all three had distinguished themselves as being wise, trustworthy, and excellent at whatever job they were given.

King Nebuchadnezzar was distressed. In one way, he respected the three Hebrews, but they had also directly disobeyed his law. So, he gave them a second chance to bow before him, and all would be forgiven.

Their faith-filled response is recorded in Daniel 3:17-18:

> "If we are thrown into the blazing furnace, the God we serve is able to deliver us from it, and he will deliver us from Your Majesty's hand. But even if he does not, we want you to know, Your Majesty, that we will not serve your gods or worship the image of gold you have set up." (NIV)

Wow! When I read their response, I am amazed by their unwavering confidence in God. I mean, I don't know if you've ever touched a hot stove burner before when cooking, but it hurts! The last time I did it, I immediately yanked my hand away, but the damage had been done. I can't even imagine being thrown into a raging inferno. Their faith is rock solid.

But what I really love in that passage is when they say, "But even if he doesn't." That shows such a deep-gut gratitude to God that, even if he didn't rescue them, they'd count it all joy to serve him anyway.

I wish I could say that my mind runs to, "But even if he doesn't," as soon as trouble sets in, but maybe like you, I find myself thinking, "*What if God doesn't?*"

Have you ever thought, "What if God doesn't heal me? What if he doesn't help me? What if he doesn't take care of this issue?"

I've found in my life that I love God and am devoted to him, but my trust wanes a bit over time. I attribute this to me forgetting about the many times that God has given me victory over problems in the past. I forget about the multitude of blessings that God has given me and tend to focus on the bad things that happened years ago.

STOP

As I'm writing this chapter, I've been given a month's sabbatical from our church. I am very grateful for this long and refreshing pause in my life. But I was also like, "What do I do?" My days are always filled with responsibilities, so to just stop is quite an odd experience for me.

So what did I do?

I learned from one of my mentors to keep a gratitude journal. She said to journal each day and to write down the victories–the times that God brought me through my many years of ministry.

Each morning, after I dropped my son off at school, I drove back home and wrote in my journal what I was grateful for that day. And as I started writing, I started remembering how God had helped me over and over throughout my life. After journaling, I'd sit back and read about God's generous blessings in my life and just smile.

He's always with me, and that promise is for *you*, too! God is always with you!

All through the physical issues I spoke about in the beginning of this chapter, God was with me, and he is with you through your challenges, difficulties, and disappointments, too.

And he was with Shadrach, Meshach, and Abednego, too!

At the end of Daniel, Chapter 3, the three Hebrews refused to obey the king's orders, and in a flight of rage, he had his guards to bind their hands and feet and throw them into the furnace that had been stoked to a temperature so high that it killed the guards as they threw Shadrach, Meshach, and Abednego inside!

After a while, curiosity got to King Nebuchadnezzar. Something about their unshakeable faith in their God wouldn't leave him alone. So, he looked inside the furnace, and instead of seeing three skeletons lying on the ground in the flames, the king saw them walking around!

And they weren't alone! Astonished, Nebuchadnezzar remarked that a fourth person was in the furnace with them and that he looked like a "son of the gods." I believe 100% that the fourth person was the true Son of God, Jesus.

Just like the three Hebrews, there is someone walking alongside you in whatever fiery trial you are going through right now and will go through in the future. His name is Jesus. We might not be thankful for the circumstances, but we can be grateful that Jesus is with us.

It Is Well

Horatio Spafford was a businessman in Chicago in the 1800s. He and his family were to voyage on an ocean liner to Europe together, but because he needed to attend to some business that came up just before their launch date, he sent his wife and four daughters ahead. He bid them all a quick farewell because he knew he'd see them soon.

In a few days, he was finishing up his business dealings when he received an urgent telegram from his wife. Grasping the small paper in his hands, he stared at the short message of only six words in all caps and re-read it many times. He was so shocked, he couldn't move.

The telegram read, "SAVED ALONE, WHAT SHALL I DO?"

He learned that the ship his family was on had collided with another ship and sank. His wife, Anne, had gathered the children with her in one of the lifeboats, but by the time they were found, the children had passed.

Without wasting any more time, Horatio boarded a ship to rendezvous with his wife. As the ship he was on passed near the waters of the disaster, he started penning the words to what would become one of the most famous hymns: "It Is Well with My Soul."

Read out loud the opening lines of this song below, and hear the mix of pain and gratitude in Horatio's voice:

> When peace like a river attendeth my way, when sorrow like sea billows roll, whatever my lot, thou hast taught me to say, it is well, it is well with my soul.

I can't even grasp what it feels like to lose one child, nevertheless *all* a person's children. Yet, here he is, being gut-honest with God about his loss and sadness but still remembering that God is still God and that God is with him.

And Horatio is grateful, not for the loss of his precious children, but for the assurance that his children are now with God in heaven and that one day, he and his wife will see them again. And I can say with confidence that this family today is reunited in heaven!

Let me encourage you: When you feel afraid or life's storms have threatened to engulf you, take time to stop, pray, write down your fears, and then write down what you are grateful for. Trust me, coming from a person who has struggled with fear many times in life; the more you focus on how God has blessed you and what you are grateful for, the more your fears will shrink and fade into the background and lose their power over you.

Chapter 5

Love Completely through Gratitude

from Jeff

Anthony Ray Hinton spent 30 years on death row, much of that time in solitary confinement with only an hour a day to leave his dismal five-by-seven-foot cell. Over the years, he became a friend and counselor to other inmates during those brief moments out of his cell. He even befriended death row guards.

So what was his crime? What had he done to have his freedom taken from him and to face the ultimate punishment of execution?

Actually, Anthony hadn't done anything. He had been falsely accused of a crime in 1985 and found guilty of murder. For 30 years, he maintained that he was innocent. Finally, the Supreme Court heard his case, and the justices unanimously ruled that he had been wrongly convicted and set him free.

In a *60 Minutes* interview, Anthony was asked if he was angry at the people who put him in jail. Anthony astonished the interviewer when he replied that he had forgiven them all.

After a pause, the interviewer continued with, "But they took 30 years of your life–how can you not be angry?"

Anthony's next reply showed even more wisdom than his first answer. "If I'm angry and unforgiving," he said, "they will have taken the rest of my life."

He went on to describe how he no longer takes anything for granted. If it rains, he's happy to feel the raindrops on his skin. If it's sunny and hot, he's happy to see another day. Now, he looks at life through the lens of gratitude and finds blessings everywhere to give thanks for.

But, There Are These People...

One of the characteristics of life that we all have to deal with is relationships. Even though Anthony Hinton spent years in solitary confinement in prison, he ended up encountering people and befriended many of them.

We all know people that it can be hard to get along with. We may work with them, run into them at school, see them in stores, and even sit down to dinner with them.

I believe that we can adapt gratitude to help us get along better with just about anybody. Let me show you how.

Accept Them

Would you agree with me that almost everybody wants to be accepted?

Most of us have seen firsthand the ridiculous behavior that some people have adopted just to be a part of the "in crowd." You may even be thinking right now of some of the crazy things that you've done in your life to try to win acceptance from a group of people.

And if you think that it's just kids and teens that do strange things to try to impress their peers, let me be the first to testify that adults do it, too!

If you don't believe me, just pull up any social media site, and you'll see example after example of people trying to be someone else just to fit in.

So if people already have this built in tendency to want to fit in, what if we flip it around and offer some loving gratitude and acceptance to them in the first place?

Now, I'm not talking about a touchy, feely love here–you know, that type that makes you feel all fuzzy inside. Nope, not that. I'm talking about the kind of love that the Bible defines in 1 Corinthians 13:4:

> Love is patient, love is kind. It does not envy, it does not
> boast, it is not proud. (NIV)

Patience. Oh boy, if you're having a hard time getting along with someone right now, patience might be the last thing on your mind. But I find it fascinating that the very definition of love begins with patience.

Being *impatient* with someone can say, "I don't have time for you. I don't respect you. I don't need you. I wish I could change you."

Ah, Family Life

Right from the start, I fell into impatience toward my family as a young father, husband, and leader. I came from a family that was *driven*–like I always had to be doing something and always had something to prove.

Then there's my sweet wife, Rhonda, who is very laid back, easy going, and not in much of a rush. Our personalities are polar opposites; so, of course, we married!

I confess that for the first ten years of our marriage, I did everything I could to change her. I wanted to make her more like me. I was a driven person who wanted her to step up and be that same driven person.

But despite all of my pushing for her to change, I was only successful in driving us apart and making us miserable.

So what changed for us? How did we come back together after slowly walking apart?

Very importantly, we went to counseling. Through a counselor's outside perspective, both of us started seeing our relationship very differently. Rhonda started to understand where I was coming from, and maybe even more important, I started accepting Rhonda for who she was.

And here's something about relationships I learned through the process. Whether we're talking about family members, friends, co-workers, or classmates, we're not going to like about 20% of their ideas, traits, and behavior. Even in the best relationships, this still happens. And it's that 20% that we will want to change or even *attempt* to change.

Now, I'm not talking about illegal or immoral behavior here with this 20%. That's a whole other issue. I'm talking about 20% of everyday decisions or actions that you don't like and the other person does.

So what if we flipped this picture over and emphasized the 80% of the person that we like? What if we intentionally started focusing on the 80% of the traits that we share?

Show people love by patiently accepting them, and you'll be well on your way to developing deep and meaningful relationships with people in all areas of your life.

Fight Right

Raise your hand if you've ever had a sharp disagreement or argument with someone you love.

Wow, look at all of those hands!

Although friendships will experience strong disagreements at times–some more than others–it's in families and particularly in marriages that some of the harshest arguments can take place. Think about it: We see coworkers, classmates, and friends for a limited time and then go home.

If we're not careful, we can bring our frustrations, foul mood, and anger from work, school, and our friendships home to our family. It's ironic and sad that we can end up treating the very people we love worse than we would treat a stranger we meet for the first time.

I believe that disagreements are inevitable in all relationships. So when they do happen, be prepared to "fight right." Now, obviously, I do not mean to engage in a physical fight; do not do that! And if abuse is going on in the home, please seek help. The National Domestic Violence hotline number is 1-800-799-7233, and it is free, confidential, and staffed 24/7.

Your home should be a safe place of love and mutual respect. So here are four ways to keep your disagreements and arguments from getting out of hand.

1.   Guard your mouth

One morning, I was at the gym. It was just a regular day, but my words and actions almost got me pummeled!

As I walked around the room, heading to a workout station, I noticed a large, strongly-built man punching the daylights out of a punching bag in the corner. I stopped a moment and just watched his frenetic energy explode with each series of punches he slammed into the bag. He shuffled his feet in a rhythmic dance as he "fluttered" around the punching bag.

I thought, "I wouldn't want to get in that guy's way," and I sat down at one of the arm machines and began my routine.

A few minutes later, I saw movement out of the corner of my eye. It was the boxer, and he was going to pass by me. Part of the reason I work out at this gym is to get to know people and to invite them to church. So I thought I would stand up and greet him.

But me being me, I wasn't content with just saying, "Hi, how ya' doin'?" I jumped up from my seat, blocked his path, and raised my hands in a boxing stance. Jokingly I said, "Don't mess with me; I watched *Rocky* last night!"

I instantly realized that I had made a horrible mistake as I watched a look of murderous rage shoot across his face. His nostrils flared, and I suddenly felt like my heart was in my throat. I thought, "Oh, Lord! I've just challenged a boxer to fight me!"

In a low, stern voice, he growled, "I'm not messing with nobody." Then he pushed past me and continued on his way. I sat back down and breathed out a long sigh of relief.

Words matter and are powerful! I should've remembered the counsel of Proverbs 18:21:

> The tongue has the power of life and death. (NIV)

Before you end up saying something you'll regret, especially to your spouse, children, or parents, pay close attention to what you are saying. Here's an important saying to remember:

Change your tone; change your home.

I actually saw the same boxer again the next day at the gym. This time, as I passed by him, I kept my words simple, just saying *hello* and *how are you doing* in a friendly tone. The end results were infinitely better as he glanced up at me and answered, "Fine."

Another verse that advises guarding your mouth is James 1:19, which says:

> My dear brothers and sisters: You must be quick to listen,
> slow to speak, and slow to get angry. (NLT)

Listening is a great way to show someone that you love and respect them. Unfortunately, I've watched over the years as it seems that people listen less and less to others. Instead, they just seem to let whatever words come to their minds, fly out of their mouths, raw, unfiltered, and unapologetic about who they hurt. This is completely the opposite of how James teaches us to behave.

If you need further proof that we should listen more than we speak, just look in the mirror. 99% of you will have two ears and one mouth. I believe that God built our bodies this way because he wanted us to listen twice as much as we talk.

In fact, if you're a talker, I double-dog dare you to set one day this week to intentionally listen a whole lot more and talk a whole lot less and see how the day goes. I triple-dog dare you!

2. Attack the problem, not the person

Have you ever found yourself arguing with someone you love over the same thing over and over? It may feel like you're stuck in this sad cycle and not able to get out. And whatever the issue is, one or both people can end up feeling unloved, attacked, and unwanted.

Ephesians 4:15 has been used by some people to defend "speaking the truth" in any way they want. They claim that people should just speak their minds, because to them, it's the "truth."

But I want to take a moment to point out what Ephesians 4:15 actually says:

> Instead, we will speak the truth in love, growing in every way more and more like Christ... (TEV)

Speak the truth *in love*.

The Crazy Cycle

One day, Rhonda and I had an appointment to meet with a couple who were planning their wedding. We were excited for them and looked forward to hearing about their plans over dinner.

But when we arrived at the restaurant, we didn't see any sign of them. Rhonda and I waited outside for a while, and just as I pulled out my phone to check on the couple, the bride-to-be walked up. Her face was red with tears and anger.

Rhonda immediately went to her and asked if she was all right.

Following Rhonda, I stood with them as the bride-to-be announced, "I'm sorry, but we're not getting married."

Rhonda and I were shocked. We asked the woman to come inside the restaurant. We sat in a booth, and as Rhonda and I started listening to the bride-to-be, she revealed that her fiancé was actually still waiting in the car.

Rhonda and I gave each other a look, and I asked our guest across the table, "Do you think he would come into the restaurant and talk with us?"

The bride-to-be sighed, snatched up her phone, and tapped out a short text.

Sure enough, in a few moments, the groom-to-be entered the restaurant and joined us at the table. As the couple sat next to each other, I could see the tension between them. Like I've done many times before, I simply asked, "So, what's going on?"

The two immediately launched into an energized, back-and-forth description of their turbulent relationship–the disagreements, the misunderstandings, the fights, and so on.

After listening for a while, I asked, "Why are you two still together?"

And do you know what both of them said? They said that they were still together because they loved each other! In my mind, I thought, "Well, if they love each other, there's still hope for their relationship!"

As they continued sharing about their breakups and makeups, I realized that they were trapped in what I call *The Crazy Cycle*.

If you're dating or married, this may sound familiar. The couple would argue by texting each other. Each new text would escalate their anger at the other person. Then they'd call each other and argue over the phone. By the time they actually *saw* each other again, the argument had exploded into a full-scale war of hurtful words that both people would regret later.

Finally, one of them would feel awful enough to apologize, and the other person, just wanting all of it to be over with, would accept and say, "We're good." But in reality, the argument was just waiting to explode again down the road since the *actual problem* hadn't been resolved.

To break out of the crazy cycle, the couple has to fix the problem and stop fixing the blame. If you're feeling right now like your marriage is caught in a storm and you feel it's about to be dashed on the rocks, the most valuable advice I can give you is for both of you to seek professional help from a counselor.

And let me tell you, Rhonda and I were caught in the crazy cycle for years! We loved each other dearly, but we were so different from each other that we were literally pulling our marriage apart!

We were stuck. We knew something needed to be fixed, but we didn't know what to do; so we just kept fixing the blame on each other. This is where a professional counselor can really help. They have an outside perspective that a couple caught in the crazy cycle can't see.

And being totally transparent with you, if Rhonda and I had not gone to marriage counseling years back, I don't know if we'd still be together today. God can't help you with a problem that you are unwilling to admit you have, and you will never love completely through gratitude until you stop blaming and shaming each other.

Don't confuse the person with the problem. Fix the problem, not the blame.

3. Don't drag past problems into your present problem

I heard of a couple who went to see a marriage counselor. The counselor asked them what they thought their biggest problem was. The wife responded, "He doesn't communicate with me."

Then the counselor glanced at the husband and asked him the same question. The husband snorted, "She gets historical!"

The counselor replied, "I think you mean hysterical."

The husband shook his head, "No, I mean *historical*. Every time we have a disagreement, she brings up everything that I've ever done wrong."

The counselor sighed, nodded, and jotted down on his notepad, "Here we go again."

Do You Remember When You...

I confess that for years, when I found myself arguing with someone, I would suddenly remember all kinds of times in the past when they had let me down or hurt me. Sometimes I even saw myself as some kind of lawyer, calling up a list of all kinds of past failings, as I argued my case before a judge.

Couples, do *not* do this!

As soon as one of you becomes historical, chances greatly increase that the other person will become hysterical, and then the argument can just explode into a storm of hateful words that injures both people. This is not the way to build a strong relationship with anyone. In fact, it can ruin friendships and marriages alike.

So what do you do if you find yourself in an increasingly emotional disagreement and you're not the person bringing up the past?

I would say that your main objective should be to de-escalate the rising tension by refocusing on the issue being discussed. Just like I said earlier that we should address the problem and not attack the person, we should focus on the present problem, not on a bunch of stuff from the past.

Also, if either of your emotions are getting out of control, take a break from the discussion to breathe and calm down. That may require that both of you go to a different area of the house or outside.

When our emotions are supercharged, it hinders our ability to think clearly, and if we're trying to solve a problem, I think you'd agree with me that both people need to have a clear and calm mind. That might mean that you go take a walk for a while to clear your mind.

Once both of you have calmed, you can then start working *together* on solutions for the problem.

4. Forgive often

Many years ago, I received a letter from one of the people who attended our church. When I opened the envelope and unfolded the letter, I was shocked by his angry and hateful words. From my perspective, his take on my character and leadership were completely wrong, and it was hard for me to not feel hurt by what he said–especially since he portrayed himself as being such a "good" person in public.

I was so mad at what he'd written that I showed the letter to Rhonda and then grabbed it back. Shaking it, I proclaimed, "I'm going to keep this letter as evidence to prove that he's not a good man!"

In the letter, he'd indicated that he'd be leaving the church, and sure enough, he did. Back then, our church was small, so everybody knew everybody. For many Sundays after that, I had person after person come to me and ask me if I knew where this man was. I wanted to tell them exactly what I thought about this guy, but the Holy Spirit would whisper, "Don't do it, Jeff. Just let it go." So I'd truthfully answer, "I don't know where he is."

But you know what; I hadn't forgiven the man.

In fact, I kept that letter in a filing cabinet, ready to pull out and use as proof of his *real* character. Just like an attorney, I was ready for my counterattack in case he ever came back. I kept the letter to protect myself, but every time I thought about it, I just grew more and more bitter.

One day I was driving along, listening to a preacher on the radio, and he said something that shook me. I could feel the Holy Spirit focus my attention on these words: "You will never completely forgive someone until you destroy the evidence of the hurt they caused you."

These words echoed in my mind, and I thought of that letter sitting in my file cabinet.

When I got home, I rushed to my office, opened the file cabinet, snatched up the letter, and just as I was about to tear up, I heard bitterness rise up inside my mind. It snarled, "You don't want to destroy that letter; you need it for evidence to protect yourself."

I knew that this was not the voice of the Holy Spirit. It was my own fearful human nature shouting louder and louder for me to hold on to my unforgiveness.

I tell you, for a moment, it felt like an all-out battle was being waged inside of me between the anger and bitterness of my fallen nature and the forgiving and freeing power of the Holy Spirit.

Finally, I slammed my foot down and said to myself, "I'm doing this! I'm forgiving this guy, and I'm done with holding this grudge!" And I ripped up the letter into tiny pieces and threw them into the trash can.

Instantly, it felt like a weight lifted from my shoulders! I took a deep breath of freedom and exhaled it with a happy sigh. I had no clue how much my unforgiveness had been weighing me down!

Colossians 3:13 teaches:

> Bear with each other, and forgive each other. If someone does wrong to you, forgive that person because the Lord forgave you. (NCV)

We all make mistakes and are in need of forgiveness. It's ironic that in order to *receive* forgiveness, we need to *give* forgiveness.

What small piece of unforgiveness are you holding on to? What do you need to "rip up" and throw away? If you feel like you're letting someone off the hook for something they did to you in the past, let me assure you that by forgiving them, you're setting *yourself* free.

Who can you forgive today to start living a freer life?

Chapter 6

We Can Be Grateful
Because God Loves Us

from Chesnee

One day, I was sitting in my Christian counselor's office. I had scheduled the appointment to seek his counsel on some upcoming decisions that were perplexing me. But in the middle of our conversation, the direction of our talk changed. With a sigh, I told him, "It's easier for me to understand God's faithfulness toward me than it is for me to understand God's love for me."

My counselor paused, gave a slight nod of his head, and replied, "That's because you're a *loyalist*. To loyalists, faithfulness means a great deal to you. To me, it sounds like you have a very narrow definition of God's love."

That last sentence really hit me and got me thinking long after that session about my relationship with God and how I receive his love. You see, my top love language is *acts of service*. I love it when people do things for me, just ask my husband Danny. But on the flip side, that means that I try to show love to people by doing things for them.

And I realized that it's through this narrow lens that I've been looking at God's love toward me: God loves me because I serve him, but when I fail to serve him fully, he doesn't love me. According to Romans 8:38-39, this thinking is not right at all:

> For I am convinced that nothing can ever separate us from his love. Death can't, and life can't. The angels won't, and all the powers of hell itself cannot keep God's love away. Our fears for today, our worries about tomorrow, or where we are–high above the sky, or in the deepest ocean–nothing will ever be able to separate us from the love of God demonstrated by our Lord Jesus Christ when he died for us. (TLB)

What can separate us from God's love? Paul beautifully declares in these verses that *nothing* can separate us from God! Not death, not life, not angels, not demons, not our fears, not our worries, not our physical location–absolutely nothing can separate us from God's love for us.

And how great is this love? God's love for us is so great that it is pictured in the sacrificial death of Jesus Christ for the forgiveness of our sins on a wooden cross, hoisted up for the world to see.

How great is God's love for us? So great that Jesus chose to receive brutal agony and death to be the bridge of reconciliation, connecting us back to God, so that we can now have a relationship with God. Just as Adam and Eve's failure in the Garden broke humanity's connection with God, Jesus' victory on the cross and triumph through his resurrection restored it.

Receiving God's Love

You can never fully know God's love until you accept Jesus as your Savior. God put his love on display when his Son willingly died on the cross for our sins. He didn't die for those who are perfect, because in truth, only God is perfect. Jesus died for all of us.

If you haven't asked Jesus into your heart, to be the Savior of your life, I encourage you to do so right now. It's not hard, and it is a gift that God is offering to you right now. All you have to do is earnestly pray the following prayer and believe:

Jesus, I come to you as a sinner. I am aware that I cannot receive your love until I have a relationship with you. Please forgive me of my sins. Make me clean and help me to follow you and to turn from my ways that displease you. I want you to be the leader of my life. Thank you, God. Amen.

If you prayed this prayer, I'm so excited and happy that you've chosen to follow Jesus! You may ask, "So, what now?" Please email us at jeffdaws@sccview.net, and we'll send you some good information to help you along in your new journey.

Personalize Scripture

Here is an interesting technique that you can use when reading inspirational passages in the Bible. All that you have to do is simply replace pronouns like *you, we,* and *us* with *me* and *I*. Now to be clear here, I'm not saying to rewrite the Bible, nor am I saying that this will work in all passages.

But if you're looking for a way to make the Bible really pull you in, put yourself in the verses. Let me demonstrate. Ephesians 2:4-5 says:

> But because of his great love for us, God, who is rich in mercy, made us alive with Christ even when we were dead in transgressions–it is by grace you have been saved. (NIV)

Now insert yourself into the scene:

But because of his great love for *me*, God, who is rich in mercy, made *me* alive with Christ even when *I* was dead in transgressions–it is by grace *I* have been saved.

Did you feel the difference reading the two? I don't know about you, but when I read the verse personalized, it has so much more weight and importance to my heart. It speaks directly to me. Here are two more verses for you to practice this technique on:

> But you, Lord, are a compassionate and gracious God, slow to anger, abounding in love and faithfulness. -Psalm 86:15 (NIV)

> The Lord your God is with you, the Mighty Warrior who saves. He will take great delight in you; in his love he will no longer rebuke you, but will rejoice over you with singing. -Zephaniah 3:17 (NIV)

Let God Love Others through You

Showing love to others is a great way to feel God's love for you. Of course, some people are hard to love for a multitude of reasons. But extending love especially to these people gives us a better understanding of what it's like for God to extend love to us. When we give love to others, it changes how we perceive God's love for us.

Hang Out with More Loving People

Another personal confession, I can be kind of a *prickly* person. But being around a diversity of people at church for years has helped me to become more loving. I can't be concerned in my everyday life about what people believe or don't believe if I'm not loving toward them first. And for me, being married to one of the most loving people on this planet helps me, too. Showing love is contagious! If you don't feel like a very loving person and you'd like to change, I challenge you to get around some generous, kind-hearted people and begin your personal transformation.

"The Love of God"

I was listening to some music with my grandparents a few years ago when I heard the old hymn "The Love of God." It's been modernized a bit over the years by music groups, but I'm drawn to the song because of its powerful words.

In the early 1900s, Frederick M. Lehman was a businessman in California who made a huge mistake in a business venture and lost everything. Out of money and unable to find work in his field, he finally found a job in a Pasadena packing house. Instead of a rags to riches story, he went from riches to rags.

Every day, Lehman spent long hours on his feet packing an endless sea of oranges and lemons into crates. It was a thankless, boring, repetitive, and exhausting job, but he gave thanks for it anyway. And despite this severe turn in his life, Lehman continued to attend church regularly and prayed daily.

One Sunday night, after hearing a sermon on the love of God that morning, he was restless and couldn't sleep. Finally, Monday morning came, and he threw his covers off in frustration. He knew that it was going to be a long day, and he'd be starting it off unrested.

But as Lehman got to the packing house and started sorting oranges and lemons, words started coming to him. He grabbed whatever scraps of paper he could find and jotted down the words, but throughout the day, the words kept coming!

Out of paper scraps, he finally had to snatch up pieces of broken crates to write on.

With the work day at an end, Lehman traveled home and gathered together the odd assortment of scribbled papers and crate pieces. As he transferred and organized the hastily written words onto a fresh piece of paper, he realized that it was a song.

He scooped up his newly-written lyrics and began plunking out a tune on his piano to match with them. Through the creative process, Lehman finished the music for the song, but one problem remained. Songs of that time needed at least three verses, and he only had two.

Then he remembered a poem that someone had given him years before. He kept the poem on a card that he used as a bookmark. Rushing over to the book, he pulled out the card and read.

According to tradition, the words came from a cell wall in a prison some 200 years ago. It is not known why the prisoner wrote them on the wall of his cell or if the words were his or someone else's. Obviously, they meant something deep to him because he would see them day after day.

In time, the prisoner died, and his cell was to be repainted. When the painters showed up, one was so impressed by the words that he jotted them down and thereby preserved them for future generations.

Lehman applied the words from the poem to his music and was happily surprised to find that they fit! I've included the words from the first and third verses and the chorus below for you to reflect on this vivid description of God's love.

Verse 1

The love of God is greater far
Than tongue or pen can ever tell;
It goes beyond the highest star,
And reaches to the lowest hell;
The guilty pair, bowed down with care,
God gave His Son to win;
His erring child He reconciled,
And pardoned from his sin.

Verse 3

Could we with ink the ocean fill,
And were the skies of parchment made,
Were every stalk on earth a quill,
And every man a scribe by trade;
To write the love of God above
Would drain the ocean dry;
Nor could the scroll contain the whole,
Though stretched from sky to sky.

Chorus

Oh, love of God, how rich and pure!
How measureless and strong!
It shall forevermore endure—
The saints' and angels' song.

The love of God is so great that we literally cannot fully comprehend it! And because of God's unending love for us, we can be grateful no matter what we go through. As for me, I will spend the rest of my life exploring the love of God, always being surprised by the discovery of its new depths. And I encourage you to do the same.

We can be grateful because God loves us.

Chapter 7

Expressing Gratitude

from Jeff

How many times have you thought of expressing gratitude to a parent, child, brother, or sister but didn't follow through and said nothing?

In my earlier years of marriage and parenthood, I would see Rhonda or my children doing something great, and in my mind, I would be like, "THAT'S AMAZING! I LOVE YOU SO MUCH! I'M SO GRATEFUL FOR YOU!"

But many times, what Rhonda and my kids heard was _____ (*silence*).

Growing up, I traveled back and forth between my parents' houses, and as I grew older, more siblings came along. There were a lot of us, and we had a lot of chores to keep up with to help out our household.

In those days, each of my parents may have had grateful thoughts toward us for the work we did, but our work was mostly *expected* not verbally thanked. Since my dad worked a full-time job during the day and then a part-time job at night, I eventually figured out that he would show me gratitude by letting me spend time in his shed with him as he worked on small engines.

But this was still unspoken, and there were times I wished he'd just say how much he appreciated me out loud.

You may know exactly how this feels.

1. Silence crushes gratitude

Fast forward back to my early years of parenting, and I was making the same mistake of thinking good things toward my family but not saying them. I thought I was doing a great job as a husband and father–*thought*, being the key word there.

But it was when I started speaking out gratitude to Rhonda, Katelyn, and Tyler that the atmosphere at home really changed. I could feel love grow among us as I said to each of them, "I love you."

Before Bed

Several years ago, I was at a men's spiritual retreat. We were in between activities, sitting around talking in random groups, and the man who was leading worship for the event came and sat down next to me. I didn't know him, and I think he sat down next to me just because the chair was available.

We chatted only for a short time before he stood up and went to prepare for the next activity, but in that brief moment, he taught me something that I will forever remember.

He said that he and his wife always held hands and said a prayer before they went to bed each night. Even if they were upset with each other for something that happened during that day, they made it a point to at least hold hands and say the Lord's Prayer before they went to sleep.

This idea was revolutionary to me; I couldn't wait to get home to tell Rhonda about it!

When I finally got back home and finished unloading the car, I slid up to Rhonda in the kitchen and with a grin said, "Hey, I've got a great idea!"

She gave me a hesitant smile and replied, "O-okay..."

Before she had a chance to escape, I blurted out, "I think we should hold hands and pray every night!"

A comical expression flashed across her face as she backed a little bit away from me. She was used to me returning from seminars and conventions with all kinds of new ideas that I wanted to put into action immediately, but this one took her a moment to process.

She echoed with a chuckle, "You want to hold hands...and pray every night?"

"Yes!" I confirmed.

"Really?"

"Yes!" I repeated enthusiastically.

I could see Rhonda weighing out the idea in her mind. Finally, she nodded with a smile and replied, "Okay, Jeff...BUT, I don't want to pray ALL night!"

For over eight years now, Rhonda and I have held hands before we go to bed and said a prayer of gratitude over each other. My prayer over her goes like this:

> Dear God, thank you for Rhonda. She is a wonderful wife, a wonderful mother, and a great person to do life with. Lord, give her what she needs, even things that I don't know about. Thank you, God, for Rhonda.

Her prayer over me goes something like this:

> God, thank you for Jeff. He is a good husband who always takes care of me. He is a good father and pastor. Bless him and guide him as he leads us. Thank you for Jeff.

And let me tell you, taking just a few minutes each day, every day before we go to bed to say a prayer of gratitude over each other has woven our hearts together deeper than anything else that we have ever said or done. And even when we're irritated with each other–because we *do* get irritated with each other at times–we still hold hands and pray.

We know where we stand. We know that both of us value each other more than anyone else on this planet, and that truth gives us such assurance that we can work through anything together with God in the center of our relationship!

Show gratitude toward your family. Tell them how much you love and value them now. Don't wait to say these things at a funeral. Tell them now! And if you're married, I challenge you to hold hands and pray over each other before you go to bed each night. It will only take five minutes, but it could be the best thing you ever do to strengthen your relationship!

2. Entitlement crushes gratitude

Entitlement has been used a lot recently in news articles, research studies, and social media posts. One generation says that another generation is "entitled." But what would you think if I told you that *entitlement* is not a new concept?

How old would you say it is? Twenty years? Fifty years? A hundred years? Two hundred years?

What if I told you that I see evidence of it having been around since the very beginning?

In Genesis, Chapter 2, we find Adam and Eve in the Garden of Eden experiencing paradise. They literally have everything they need (and more!) all around them: abundant food, fresh water, a comfortable climate, companionship with each other, and daily face-to-face visits with God.

They had no bills, no problems, no sickness, no pain, no sorrow, no tears, no death, no anxiety, and no fear! The only work they had to do was to tend the beautiful garden that they lived in and harvest the food they ate.

And get this: their bodies were the perfect, original versions of ours. They never tired and never aged. They were continuously re-energized to the point that they could enjoy working all day long and never break a sweat. Wow!

And so for all of this, they showed gratitude toward God, right?

Well…maybe at first.

But somewhere along the way, it seems that they started taking their extraordinary blessings for granted and started drifting away from God's original instructions.

How do we know this?

Well, in Genesis 3:3, we learn from Eve herself that God gave her and Adam free reign of the garden except for one thing: they couldn't touch or eat the fruit from the tree in the center of the garden. It was strictly forbidden!

But even before her infamous encounter with the serpent at the Tree of the Knowledge of Good and Evil, Eve may have already been sliding from a spirit of gratitude toward God for his tremendous blessings to a "ho-hum" attitude of entitlement.

I wonder how many times she and Adam strolled by the forbidden tree with its tempting fruit. I wonder if they thought, "This garden is ours. We can do whatever we want."

What we definitely know is that Eve eventually went to where she shouldn't have been, and the fateful moment is recorded in Genesis 3:1-7:

> Now the serpent was more crafty than any of the wild animals…and he said to the woman, "Did God really say, 'You must not eat from any tree in the garden?'" The woman said to the serpent, "We may eat fruit from the trees in the garden, but God did say, 'You must not eat fruit from the tree that is in the middle of the garden, and you must not touch it, or you will die.'" "You will

not surely die," the serpent said to the woman. "For God knows that when you eat of it your eyes will be opened, and you will be like God, knowing good and evil." When the woman saw that the fruit of the tree was good for food and pleasing to the eye, and also desirable for gaining wisdom, she took some and ate it. She also gave some to her husband, who was with her, and he ate it. Then the eyes of both of them were opened, and they realized they were naked; so they sewed fig leaves together and made coverings for themselves.

The Devil is a deceiver, and just like the serpent here, twists the truth to convince us to do wrong. In a way, Adam and Eve's rebellion said, "We don't need God; we know better than him!" But their feelings of entitlement didn't last long.

In a split second, they realized that they had done wrong, panicked, and ran to hide themselves from each other and from God. Entitlement says, "You owe me." Gratitude says, "I appreciate you."

Ingratitude wasn't just a problem in the Garden of Eden. Check out this prophecy in 2 Timothy 3:1-3:

In the last days there will be violent periods of time. People will be selfish and love money. They will brag, be arrogant, and use abusive language. They will curse their parents, show no gratitude, have no respect for what is holy, and lack normal affection for their families. (GW)

We have to be vigilant that we don't slide into a lackadaisical mindset of entitlement. It crushes the attitude of gratitude.

3. Kindle hope with gratitude

Gratitude is a choice. But many times, we don't feel like choosing gratitude. During any given day, we may feel down, stressed, and irritated about all kinds of things. But I'm challenging you to be intentional and to choose being grateful especially when your day is not going well.

Why? Well consider what Colossians 3:17 says:

> And whatever you do, whether in word or deed, do it
> all in the name of the Lord Jesus, giving thanks to God
> the Father through him. (NIV)

I've found throughout my life that when I'm feeling overwhelmed and down, lifting up God by expressing my gratefulness and thankfulness to him lifts me up. When I get my mind off of what is happening here on this planet and I focus my attention on God through worship, HOPE sparks within me.

Suddenly, I understand that I am not alone facing the battle. God is with me, and by praising him, I'm fanning the flames of hope!

When I was a young Christian, we sang a hymn at church on many Sunday mornings that was taken from Psalm 100:4, which says:

> Enter his gates with thanksgiving and his courts with
> praise: give thanks to him and praise his name. (NIV)

In the New Testament, 1 Thessalonians 5:16-18 echoes this same emphasis on giving gratitude to God through praise:

> Rejoice always, pray continually, give thanks in all
> circumstances; for this is God's will for you in Christ
> Jesus. (NIV)

I can tell you from experience, life can be downright hard, heartbreaking, confusing, and scary at times. But God counsels us to give thanks to him anyway, in all circumstances–*not for* all circumstances– but *in all* circumstances. Raise up gratitude to God, and he will raise up hope within you.

4. Heart healing comes through gratitude

When my father was fifty years old, he was rushed to the hospital to have emergency surgery on his heart. To conduct the surgery, the surgeons had to cut open my father's chest. Afterward, my father appeared to heal well. As you'd expect, he was left with a long scar down his chest from the procedure, but he was also left with something unexpected.

Perhaps from how the nerves in the skin were cut or how they healed made my dad super sensitive to any touch along the incision. Any time his shirt came into contact with the scar, he'd grimace and pull the shirt away from his skin. The process became so routine to him, he frequently pulled his shirt away from his chest without even thinking about it.

The surgery happened years ago, but its effects still linger.

To some degree, we all have wounded hearts. We've been hurt by others, and we've hurt ourselves. If we're not careful, we can view life through the wounds of our past and go into a "protective" mode, pulling away from people, or into a "destructive" mode, spewing anger on people.

And here's the kicker: We probably don't even know why we act the way we do!

Just like my father automatically pulls his shirt away from the incision, we frequently walk through life on autopilot.

Right now, you might be holding people at a distance–even the people you love–without realizing it, because at some point, you were hurt by someone you trusted.

Good Medicine

Rather than living on autopilot, there is a better way. You can start by focusing on the positive. Proverbs 17:22 (NLT) gives us this gem of wisdom:

> A cheerful heart is good medicine, but a broken spirit
> saps a person's strength.

There have been many studies that have proven that people who think cheerful thoughts feel happier throughout the day. Wow! It's not rocket science, people!

Thinking cheerful thoughts bring a refreshing rejuvenation of our hearts and minds. According to the Bible, it's literally like a medicine to our bodies and our lives!

Behind a Song

A while back, I was listening to Christian music, and the song "Raise a Hallelujah" came on. I was immediately pulled into the power of the lyrics and wondered about the story behind the song, and I was amazed at what I learned.

Joel Taylor of Bethel Music and his wife Jamie experienced a crisis that none of us would want to go through. Their two-year-old son Jaxon had not been feeling well and was suddenly getting worse. Sensing that something was very wrong, Joel and Jamie took their son to the hospital.

There, his condition continued to decline as doctors diagnosed him with an aggressive E-coli infection that had spread to his internal organs. To the shock of the parents, the doctors revealed that Jaxon's kidneys were shutting down and that dialysis and blood transfusions would be required just to stabilize him.

At this point, the doctors were very grim as the infection continued to spread despite treatments. If Jaxon had been my child, I'm sure I would've felt overwhelmed in so many ways. I would've prayed and prayed over my son, just like Joel and Jamie did over Jaxon. And I probably would've wondered, "God, where are you? We really need your help now."

Unknown to Joel and Jamie, the situation was to get even worse. Just a short time later, their four-year-old daughter Addie also became gravely ill with the same infection. With both of their children hospitalized and not expected to survive, Joel and Jamie cried out for help from the Christian community. Message of their gut-wrenching dilemma spread like wildfire on social media, and soon, an army of countless Christians from all over the world were praying for the recovery of Jaxon and Addie.

Songwriters and friends of the family, Jonathan and Melissa Helser, were also praying fervently for the healing of Jaxon and Addie. One fateful night, Jonathan received a text that Jaxon wasn't going to make it. He and his wife began praying again, and suddenly Jonathan felt a new song stirring inside of him. The beginning words were, "I'll raise a hallelujah, in the presence of my enemies."

Urgently, the Helsers wrote out the song lyrics and gathered with their music team to finish what would become the very anthem of Jaxon and Addie's fight to survive. In the Bible, 2 Corinthians 10:4 states:

> The weapons we fight with are not the weapons of the world. On the contrary, they have divine power to demolish strongholds. (NIV)

How can someone fight a spiritual battle? With spiritual weapons! Praise, worship, gratitude, quoting Scripture, singing about God and his goodness, and of course prayer are how we can fight spiritual battles. And that's what countless Christians did as they stood in the gap for Jaxon and Addie.

After several weeks in the hospital, both children did not die but recovered. Can you imagine the joy both of those parents felt as they took their children back home? Joel said, "God's timing often doesn't make sense until you look back to see that mountains were climbed and canyons were crossed on no strength of your own."

Both children experienced a miraculous healing and are perfectly healthy today! To that I say, "Hallelujah!"

So for you, in your life, when you encounter mountains that seem too high to climb or dark valleys too low to make it through, I encourage you to turn to gratitude, praise, worship, Bible reading, singing, and prayer to fight spiritual battles and to receive healing for your heart.

Raise a hallelujah!

Other books by Jeff Daws
Available from online retailers

Life is hard! Relationships fall apart, loved ones pass, and the financial pressures of just trying to survive can crush you. But even in the gloom of life's unrelenting challenges, there is hope! In this book, *Your Opportunity for a Better Life*, learn 9 practical, powerful keys that will help you transform your life from failure to success

Unleash the power of prayer to revolutionize your life! *The Perfect Prayer* will help you deepen your relationship with God. No longer will you get stuck wondering how to pray or if your prayers are heard. *The Perfect Prayer* is your guide to getting God's attention!

"From my many years of ministering to people of all walks of life, I've witnessed a recurring, self-defeating pattern of people getting stuck in their lives. They want their situation to be different but do not know how to move FORWARD. After much reflection upon my own struggles, failures, and victories, I've filled *Change Forward* with powerful and practical principles to help people maximize change in their life to catapult themselves out of their regrets, self-negativity, and unfulfilled dreams so that they can move forward into a vibrant, successful life!" – Jeff Daws

CPSIA information can be obtained
at www.ICGtesting.com
Printed in the USA
JSHW010452130822
29143JS00006BA/10